My Flag

Ellen K. Mitten

ROURKE PUBLISHING

www.rourkepublishing.com

www.rourkepublishing.com

PHOTO CREDITS: Cover: © Sean Locke, © Jani Bryson; Title Page: © Images by Barbara; Page 3: © narvikk; Page 5: © Brent Melton; Page 7: © Sean Locke; Page 9: © Buttershug; Page 17: © Nicole S. Young; Page 19: © Michael Gatewood; Page 21, 22: © Catherine Yeulet; Page 23: © Brent Melton, © Images by Barbara

Edited by Meg Greve

Cover design by Renee Brady
Interior design by Tara Raymo

Library of Congress Cataloging-in-Publication Data

Mitten, Ellen.
My flag / Ellen K. Mitten.
    p. cm. -- (Little world social studies)
Includes bibliographical references and index.
ISBN 978-1-61590-327-6 (Hard Cover) (alk. paper)
ISBN 978-1-61590-566-9 (Soft Cover)
1. Flags--United States--Juvenile literature. I. Title.
CR113.M5187 2011
929.9'2--dc22
                                    2010009262

Rourke Publishing
Printed in the United States of America, North Mankato, Minnesota
033010
033010LP

www.rourkepublishing.com - rourke@rourkepublishing.com
Post Office Box 643328 Vero Beach, Florida 32964

My **flag** is the flag of the United States of America.

My flag is red, white, and blue.

Flag Facts

The United States flag flies every day from town halls, post offices, schools, government buildings, and sports fields.

5

The color red is a **symbol** for courage.

Flag Facts

People hang the flag during the day and in good weather. If it is on a pole, it must be at the very top. It may never touch the ground.

The color white is a symbol for generosity and goodness.

The color blue is a symbol for fairness.

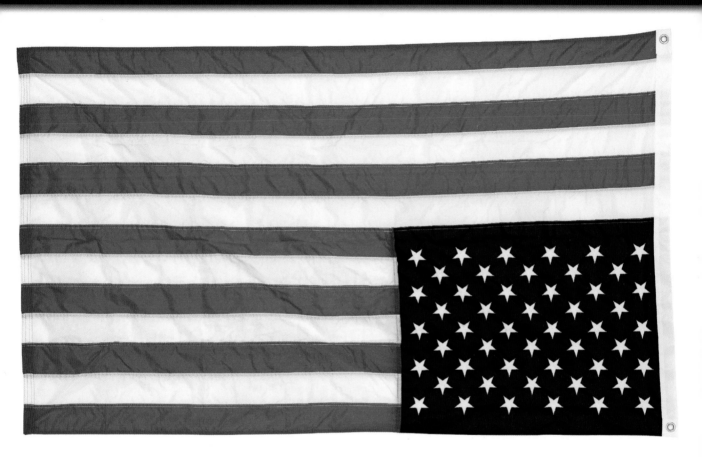

Flag Facts

A flag hung upside down is a signal that a threat or danger is close.

My flag has 13 stripes. The 13 stripes stand for the 13 original **colonies** in my **country**.

New Hampshire

Massachusetts

New York

Rhode Island

Connecticut

Pennsylvania

New Jersey

Delaware

Maryland

Virginia

North Carolina

South Carolina

Georgia

13 Original Colonies
(1776-1789)

Territories

Disputed areas

My flag has 50 stars. The 50 stars stand for each of the 50 **states** in my country.

Many children in school salute the United States flag every day while saying the Pledge of Allegiance.

The Pledge of Allegiance

I pledge allegiance to the flag
of the United States of America,
and to the republic for which it stands,
one nation under God, indivisible,
with liberty and justice for all.

On June 14, people across my country fly their flags. This is a national holiday called Flag Day.

My flag stands for freedom for all **Americans**. My flag gives my country great pride.

Picture Glossary

 **Americans** (uh-MER-uh-kuhns): People who are citizens of the United States.

 **colonies** (KOL-uh-neez): Land that has been settled by people from another country and is controlled by that country.

 **country** (KUHN-tree): Any place in the world with its own borders and government.

 **flag** (FLAG): A piece of cloth with special designs and colors on it that are symbols of a country.

 **states** (STATES): Smaller areas of land that are part of a country. There are 50 states in the United States.

 **symbol** (SIM-buhl): A design or an object that stands for something else.

Index

Websites

www.flaghouse.org

www.usa-flag-site.org/history.shtml

www.kids.gov

About the Author

Ellen K. Mitten has been teaching four and five year-olds since 1995. She and her family love reading all sorts of books!

24